"As a pastor, I get asked lots of questions. I'm approached by unbelievers seeking to understand the gospel, new believers unsure about next steps, and maturing believers wanting help answering questions from their Christian family, friends, neighbors, or coworkers. It's in these moments that I wish I had a book to give them that was brief, answered their questions, and pointed them in the right direction for further study. Church Questions is a series that provides just that. Each booklet tackles one question in a biblical, brief, and practical manner. The series may be called Church Questions, but it could be called 'Church Answers.' I intend to pick these up by the dozens and give them away regularly. You should too."

Juan R. Sanchez, Senior Pastor, High Pointe Baptist Church, Austin, Texas

"Where can we Christians find reliable answers to our common questions about life together at church—without having to plow through long, expensive books? The Church Questions booklets meet our need with answers that are biblical, thoughtful, and practical. For pastors, this series will prove a trustworthy resource for guiding church members toward deeper wisdom and stronger unity."

Ray Ortlund, President, Renewal Ministries

Why Is the
Lord's Supper
So Important?

Church Questions

Why Is the Lord's Supper So Important?

Aubrey M. Sequeira

:: CROSSWAY®

WHEATON, ILLINOIS

Trade paperback ISBN: 978-1-4335-7223-4
ePub ISBN: 978-1-4335-7226-5
PDF ISBN: 978-1-4335-7224-1
Mobipocket ISBN: 978-1-4335-7225-8

Library of Congress Cataloging-in-Publication Data

Names: Sequeira, Aubrey M., author.
Title: Why is the Lord's supper so important? / Aubrey M. Sequeira.
Description: Wheaton, Il : Crossway, 2021. | Series: Church questions | Includes bibliographical references and index.
Identifiers: LCCN 2020041276 (print) | LCCN 2020041277 (ebook) | ISBN 9781433572234 (trade paperback) | ISBN 9781433572241 (pdf) | ISBN 9781433572265 (epub) | ISBN 9781433572258 (mobipocket)
Subjects: LCSH: Lord's Supper. | Lord's Supper—Biblical teaching.
Classification: LCC BV825.3 .S49 2021 (print) | LCC BV825.3 (ebook) | DDC 264/.36—dc23
LC record available at https://lccn.loc.gov/2020041276
LC ebook record available at https://lccn.loc.gov/2020041277

Crossway is a publishing ministry of Good News Publishers.

BP		30	29	28	27	26	25	24	23	22	21
15	14	13	12	11	10	9	8	7	6	5	4	3	2	1

For as often as you eat this bread and drink the cup, you proclaim the Lord's death until he comes.

1 Corinthians 11:26

The pastor finishes preaching and stands behind a table to introduce what he calls a "meal." He indicates that the church "celebrates this meal" in remembrance of what Christ has done. He mentions Jesus's body broken and his blood shed for sinners. He then gives instructions on who can and cannot participate. He prays, and a sense of solemnity fills the building as people pass around trays containing little wafers and doll-sized cups of juice. Finally, everybody eats their wafers, drinks their juice, and sings a hymn.

For the uninitiated, the Lord's Supper can feel peculiar, even strange. What just happened?

How is this a "meal"? Why do Jesus's people eat and drink this way, and how is it connected to their faith? These aren't just questions from unchurched Bob or non-Christian Ahmed visiting church on a Sunday morning. They're questions many faithful Christians either are too embarrassed to ask, or sadly, have never given much thought.

It's easy to go through the motions during the Lord's Supper. It's easy just to believe something special takes place without ever knowing *why*. It's easy to eat and drink and think that somehow Jesus is doing something for us in this moment even if we're not sure what that something is.

But if we just go through the motions, then we reduce the Lord's Supper to mere ritual and miss out on its main purpose. Jesus wants us to know what we're doing and why we do it when we eat and drink at his Supper. In this beautiful and peculiar act of worship, Jesus wants to bless us. And that blessing comes to us only as we *thoughtfully participate* in this meaning-filled meal.

Why did you pick up this little book? Maybe you've caught yourself taking the Lord's Supper without thinking about what's actually happening. Maybe you've wondered why churches even practice the Lord's Supper. Or maybe you've attended churches where the Lord's Supper is left unexplained. And now you want someone to explain *why* it's important and *how* it's relevant for your Christian life.

I want to do just that. By thinking through what Scripture says about the Lord's Supper, you will maximize your joy in this meal as you celebrate it with your church.

A Meal of Remembrance

I'm what you might call a "foodie." Having lived in both the East and the West, I love food that introduces me to new tastes and smells. I'm also fascinated by how culinary experiences can bring back memories of the past. While I lived in North America, Indian food reminded me of my mom's cooking and life back home in South India. As I now live in the Middle East, hamburgers remind me of my time in America. Food evokes feelings. Meals bring back memories. In the Lord's Supper, Jesus gives us a meal to evoke memories—to remember what he has done for us.

Do you remember Jesus's last night with his disciples? He shared one last Passover meal with his closest friends before he was betrayed, beaten, and crucified. In these final moments, Jesus gave them a meal to remember him as they celebrated God's rescue of his chosen people in the Passover. A quick flashback will help us understand.

In Genesis, God promised to bless Abraham and his family and all nations through them (Genesis 12; 15; 17; 22). Yet Exodus begins with this family—the people of Israel—living under back-breaking slavery in Egypt.

The Israelites cried out to God, and he heard their cry. He sent nine plagues to show he was the one true God, and he then sent a tenth, climactic act of judgment. He would pass through the land of Egypt and judge the Egyptians by killing every firstborn. But he would protect the firstborn of the Israelites if each household sacrificed a lamb and spread its blood around the entrances of their homes (Ex. 12:12–13).

Inside the Israelite homes, families gathered for a meal. They ate the sacrificed lamb with bitter herbs and unleavened bread, a meal that would be remembered for years to come as the Passover.

Passover became an annual event for the Israelites. God himself instituted it to remind them that he spared Israel not because they were without sin, but because of his mercy and the blood of the lamb (Ex. 12:23). Every year, generation after generation, the people of Israel remembered God's act of salvation by eating a meal (Ex. 12:24–27).

Now let's return to Passover night with Jesus and his disciples. As they celebrated the Passover one last time, commemorating God's act of salvation in the past, Jesus gave his disciples a new meal to remember:

> Now as they were eating, Jesus took bread, and after blessing it broke it and gave it to

the disciples, and said, "Take, eat; this is my body." And he took a cup, and when he had given thanks he gave it to them, saying, "Drink of it, all of you, for this is my blood of the covenant, which is poured out for many for the forgiveness of sins." (Matt. 26:26–28)

The next day, Jesus died on a cross as a substitute for his people, bearing God's wrath against sinners. God then raised Jesus from the dead in glory, and now he reigns in heaven, offering forgiveness and eternal life to all who trust in him. If you are reading this and haven't trusted in Jesus, this offer applies to you too! Turn from your sin, trust in Jesus today, and you will receive forgiveness and your life will be transformed forever.

Just like the Passover meal recalled God's rescue of Israel, the Lord's Supper reminds Jesus's people of how he's rescued us. Yet this meal commemorates a far greater salvation. The rescue from Egypt and the Passover were previews of a greater salvation. Through the death of Christ, God rescued his people from slavery to sin.

Jesus used a Passover meal to point his disciples to a new and greater Passover sacrifice—the bread representing his body and the wine representing his blood. Jesus is the Passover Lamb of God who takes away the sins of the world (John 1:29; 1 Cor. 5:7). And his Supper helps us remember his great act of salvation.

As we eat the bread and drink the cup, we remember *him*, just as he told us to: "Do this in remembrance of me" (Luke 22:19). We look back with thankful hearts to the cross.[1]

We don't need to *repeat* Jesus's sacrifice; it is perfect and needs no improvement. We need instead to *remember* what he's done and *relish* what his perfect sacrifice means for us. The bread symbolizes Jesus's body and the wine symbolizes Jesus's blood. As we eat and drink these symbols, they point us to Jesus's loving and life-giving sacrifice. The Lord's Supper, then, helps us remember the gospel tangibly with our senses:

- As you taste the bread, remember that as real as that bread is in your mouth, so real is the fact that the Son of God became a man and gave up his body for you so that you might have eternal life.

- As you taste the sweetness of the wine or grape juice, remember the sweetness of having your sins forgiven because Jesus poured out his blood for you.

As you take the Lord's Supper, remember:

- You were an enemy of God, but now you've been adopted into his family.
- You stood condemned in your sin, but now you're counted righteous.
- You were a slave to sin, but now you've been set free to serve God.
- You were dead in your sin, but now you've been made alive.
- You were headed for hell, but now you're a citizen of God's heavenly kingdom.

. . . and all of this is because of Jesus!

This act of remembering is not some mere mental activity. It's a remembering that redefines and shapes who we are. It cancels our self-centered life stories and places us inside a new and far grander narrative. It's a training exercise in living inside our new identities.

Let your heart be filled with thankfulness for the life that Jesus purchased for you through his death. That's why the Lord's Supper is sometimes called the "Eucharist"—"eucharist" comes from a Greek word that means "thanksgiving." At the Lord's Supper, we look backward with thankful hearts to the cross of our Lord Jesus.

A Meal of Togetherness

I've lived in a few countries and had the pleasure of getting to know people from different cultures. One thing I've noticed common across cultures is that families eat together. Whether it's dinner together at home or big feasts at family holidays, meals have a way of bringing families together. As we eat, we're able to look one another in the eye, share time together, and be a part of one another's lives.

The Lord's Supper is no different. Yes, it's a meal where we remember Jesus and what ne has done for us individually. But it's also a family meal where we remember Jesus *together*.

Many Christians think the Christian life is something that's just between "me and Jesus." They think the church has little or nothing to do with our personal relationship with Jesus; it's simply an optional weekly event. With this mindset, the Lord's Supper is treated like a private dinner date with Jesus: I remember what he's done for *me* in a special moment that *I'm* sharing with him. But this attitude misses the whole point, not just of the Lord's Supper but of the Christian life itself.

When Jesus died on the cross, he didn't just save a bunch of individuals with no relation to each other; he died to save a *people*. In fact, Jesus died so that sinners from all over the world—people from different ethnicities, languages, cultures, and backgrounds—would be united together in him as God's worldwide family. Jesus shed his blood so that we would become his blood-bought brothers and sisters, adopted as God's children.

Notice how these biblical texts emphasize Jesus bringing us together as a *family*:

- So then you are no longer strangers and aliens, but you are fellow citizens with the saints and *members of the household of God* (Eph. 2:19).
- That is why he is not ashamed to call them brothers, saying, "I will tell of your name to my brothers; in the midst of the congregation I will sing your praise" . . . And again, "Behold, I and the children God has given me" (Heb. 2:11–13).

When Christians call each other "brother" or "sister," it's not simply a Christian way of being warm and friendly; we're using a precious title that reflects a spiritual reality. We truly *are* brothers and sisters, and we've been made so by the blood of Jesus. He has saved us *from* the world and brought us *into* his family.

What should we do about this? We should join a church.[2] After all, Jesus calls us to live out this family relationship through membership in a local church. Local churches are groups of

Christians who commit to follow Christ's commands together:

- They gather together regularly under the preaching of God's word.
- They care for one another and live life together as the family of God.
- They recognize and affirm one another's faith through baptism and the Lord's Supper.

If you've trusted in Jesus and committed your life to him, then you should commit yourself to other Christians in a local church. In the church, you'll learn to live as a disciple of Jesus. Life together with other Christians in the local church is not optional or a bonus; it's basic obedience.

If you wanted to identify the members of my family, you could look at my marriage certificate and my children's birth certificates—or you could simply come to my home each evening and look at who is regularly seated at the table. Similarly, Jesus has given local churches baptism and the Lord's Supper to mark out who belongs to *his* family. Let me explain.

In baptism, at least two things happen: (1) a Christian publicly identifies with Jesus and his people, and (2) a church publicly affirms the believer and receives him or her into Jesus's family. At the Lord's Supper, Christians renew their commitment both to Jesus and one another; they affirm their ongoing faith in Jesus and their mutual membership in his family. Together, baptism and the Lord's Supper identify who is "in" and who is "out" in a local church—they show us who belongs to the family.

The Lord's Supper is a family meal. That's why only a church should take the Lord's Supper when gathered together. As a new Christian, I thought the Lord's Supper was something that Christians could do any time a few of them happened to be together. As an eager (and ignorant!) new Christian, I shared bread and wine with Christian roommates and even with my new bride on an airplane, believing that we were taking the "Lord's Supper" together. Regrettably, this kind of uninformed action is pretty common. Maybe you've heard how Buzz Aldrin, the second man on the moon, served himself the Lord's Supper on the moon! As "cool" as that sounds, Scripture makes it clear that the Lord's Supper is a special meal to be shared only when the church is gathered: it's our assembled-together-ness that makes it the Lord's Supper![3]

Consider how the apostle Paul corrected some self-centered Christians in Corinth. The church was a complete mess. Church members had divided into cliques around their favorite teachers and swept scandalous sin under the rug. They were confused about a host of issues ranging from marriage and divorce to worship and spiritual gifts. But one problem was so serious that it had provoked God's discipline, causing some to fall sick and even die. What problem elicited such a strong response from the Lord? They had disregarded one another at the Lord's Supper.

Some Corinthians were behaving selfishly; they wouldn't wait for one another when they celebrated the Supper. The rich members hogged all the food and guzzled all the wine before the poorer members of the church could even show up. Correcting this error, Paul repeatedly emphasized that the Corinthians needed *to gather* before celebrating the Lord's Supper:

- "*When you come together* it is not for the better but for the worse" (1 Cor 11:17).
- "*When you come together as a church*, I hear that there are divisions among you" (1 Cor. 11:18).
- "*When you come together*, it is not the Lord's supper that you eat. For in eating, each one goes ahead with his own meal. One goes hungry, another gets drunk. What! Do you not have houses to eat and drink in? Or do you despise the church of God and humiliate those who have nothing? What shall I say to you? Shall I commend you in this? No, I will not" (1 Cor. 11:20–22).
- "So then, my brothers, *when you come together* to eat, wait for one another—if anyone is hungry, let him eat at home—so that *when you come together* it will not be for judgment" (1 Cor. 11:33–34).

According to Paul, the Lord's Supper ought to be shared *together* when assembled as a church. Just like a family shares a special family meal when the family is *together*, the Lord's Supper is reserved for when the church family is together. It's not for small groups, church Bible studies, a bunch of Christians at a conference, teenagers at a camp, or even for astronauts on the moon!

But the Bible also goes one step further. The Lord's Supper is even more than the meal that identifies the members of Jesus's family. The Lord's Supper actually *makes* a group of believers in Christ into a local church.

Jesus brings us into his family through our faith in his once-for-all sacrifice. Because we're united to Christ, we're also united to one another in him. As we remember his sacrifice together at the Lord's Supper, we pledge our allegiance both to Jesus and to one another. The Lord's Supper celebrates and expresses our unity like nothing else can. It *binds us together* as the family of Christ. As we eat and drink together, we become *one*.

Let's visit Corinth again. The believers there were not only disregarding one another at the Lord's Supper, some of them were also participating in pagan meals that honored false gods. Paul cautioned the Corinthians that participating in these meals was to share in idolatry. On the flip side, to share in the Lord's Supper is to share in Christ. Paul wrote:

> The cup of blessing that we bless, is it not a participation in the blood of Christ? The bread that we break, is it not a participation in the body of Christ? Because there is one bread, we who are many are one body, for we all partake of the one bread. (1 Cor. 10:16–17)

What does this mean? It means that when we eat and drink the Lord's Supper, we're seated at the dinner table with Jesus: we *commune* with him. And because we commune with him, we also commune with one another. That's why the Lord's Supper is often called "communion." Look again at what Paul says in verse 17: Though we are many, we become *one body*, because we partake of the *one bread*. In other words, the Lord's Supper makes us one; it makes us a church.

One of the great blessings of my life is the congregation I pastor. Our church is located in a global city in the Middle East. It's composed of people from nearly fifty nationalities and even more ethnicities, cultures, and languages. By his death, Jesus has united all of us in him. When we gather as a church, we experience a foretaste of heaven, where the people Jesus has redeemed from every tribe, tongue, and nation will worship him forever (Rev. 7:9–12).

On one occasion as our church shared the Lord's Supper, my home country of India was on the brink of war with neighboring Pakistan—a conflict that had been bubbling over for decades. That morning, two men served our congregation the Lord's Supper: one was from India, and one was from Pakistan. Though their home countries were on the brink of war, these men were at peace with each other—all because of the body and blood of Jesus. They ate and drank together as members of the same family. That's what the Lord's Supper puts on display: the peace and unity that Jesus has won for us, both around his table now and around his throne forever.

So what does all this mean for you? The next time you come to the Lord's Supper, here are a few things to keep in mind:

- It's not just about you! This isn't your private, extra-special moment with Jesus; it's a special time with the family that he's brought you into.
- On a regular basis, learn more about how God has worked in the lives of other members of your church; find out how they came to know Jesus and how they've grown in the Lord. When you take the Lord's Supper, thank God for the grace in their lives as much as in yours.
- You're not only remembering what Jesus has done to save these individuals, you're celebrating the fact that he's made all of you one family. Give thanks for the blood-bought bond that unites you to Jesus and to each other. Enjoy your communion with Jesus and your church family.

A Meal of Nourishment

A few years ago, I traded my unhealthy, sedentary lifestyle for a demanding exercise regimen.

I also learned to adjust my diet to match the new (and strenuous!) demands. As I made these changes, I heard a common nutritional mantra: "Food is fuel." The idea is simple: a healthy diet supports a healthy lifestyle.

If you've walked with Jesus for any amount of time, you know the Christian life is far more strenuous and demanding than any physical exercise routine. Thankfully, Jesus fuels us with nutritious food—the food of his word and the food of his Supper. The Lord's Supper nourishes and strengthens our faith as we walk with Jesus. To understand how, we need to reflect on the terms of our relationship with God in Christ.

When Jesus died on the cross, he didn't just save us from our sins; he saved us for a relationship with God through him. In Christ, God pledged himself to us; he promised to forgive our sins, transform our lives, and give us a true and intimate knowledge of himself. He committed himself to us in what the Bible calls a "covenant."

What's a covenant? A covenant is a committed relationship marked by loyal love and faithfulness and built on binding promises. Marriage, for example, is a covenant in which a man and a woman pledge themselves to one another.

In the Old Testament, we see God enter into covenants with his people. These covenants appear at key points in the Bible's story. And yet human beings—whether Adam or God's chosen people, Israel—prove unfaithful covenant-breakers. That's why God's promise to make a "new covenant" with his people is so wonderful. He promised to establish a covenant that would be different from before:

> Behold, the days are coming, declares the LORD, when I will make a new covenant with the house of Israel and the house of Judah, not like the covenant that I made with their fathers on the day when I took them by the hand to bring them out of the land of Egypt, my covenant that they broke, though I was their husband, declares the LORD. For this is the covenant that I will make with the house of Israel

after those days, declares the LORD: I
will put my law within them, and I will
write it on their hearts. And I will be their
God, and they shall be my people. And no
longer shall each one teach his neighbor
and each his brother, saying, "Know the
LORD," for they shall all know me, from
the least of them to the greatest, declares
the LORD. For I will forgive their iniquity,
and I will remember their sin no more.
(Jer. 31:31–34)

In this text, God promised his people a new
covenant in which he would give them forgiveness of sins, obedient hearts, and an intimate
relationship with him. But this raises some huge
questions: How could God forgive his people's
sins? How would the covenant-keeping God
enter into a lasting covenant with a covenant-
breaking people?

When Jesus instituted the Lord's Supper,
he explicitly declared that he was setting up
the promised new covenant of Jeremiah 31
through his death:

And he took a cup, and when he had given thanks he gave it to them, saying, "Drink of it, all of you, for this is my blood of the covenant, which is poured out for many for the forgiveness of sins." (Matt. 26:27–28)

This cup that is poured out for you is the new covenant in my blood. (Luke 22:20)

God enters into covenant with sinners because of Jesus's sacrifice. Jesus established the new covenant by giving himself up in death, bearing the punishment we deserve, and paying for our sins by his blood. Through Jesus, we become beneficiaries of all God's new covenant promises.

What does all this have to do with the Lord's Supper? Well, the Lord's Supper points to our participation in the glorious promises of this new covenant. The Supper, like baptism, is a *sign* of the new covenant. In the Bible, covenants are usually accompanied by covenant signs. For example, we see the rainbow in God's covenant with Noah (Gen. 9:8–17), circumcision in God's covenant with Abraham (Gen. 17:9–14), and the

Passover in God's covenant with Israel. Even in marriage, the husband and wife exchange wedding rings as signs of their covenant promises. God gave us baptism and the Lord's Supper as covenant signs to remind us of his faithfulness.

By visually reminding us of God's faithfulness, the Lord's Supper nourishes our faith and feeds our souls. Think again of the new covenant promised in Jeremiah 31:31–34. Through Jesus, these promises become a reality. Remember, in the new covenant, Jesus has given us *himself*. Through our union with him, our hearts are empowered to live in faith and obedience to God's commands and in true fellowship with God. The Lord's Supper is where we taste, in more ways than one, the fulfillment of these promises.

This is why Jesus identifies the bread and the wine with himself:

> Take, eat; *this is my body*. . . . Drink of it, all of you, for *this is my blood* of the covenant, which is poured out for many for the forgiveness of sins. (Matt. 26:26–28)

In John's Gospel, although Jesus is not speaking specifically about the Lord's Supper, he describes belief in him this way:

> Truly, truly, I say to you, unless you eat the flesh of the Son of Man and drink his blood, you have no life in you. . . . Whoever feeds on my flesh and drinks my blood abides in me, and I in him. (John 6:53, 56)

Jesus uses the language of eating and drinking to point to the life-giving nature of our union with him. When we believe in Jesus, *we receive him*. At the Lord's Supper, when we eat and drink in faith, we *feed on Christ by faith*. We're lifted up to his heavenly table where we *commune* with him by faith. Just like a good smoothie supplies weary muscles with the fuel necessary for a grueling workout, the Lord's Supper replenishes our faith reserves and fuels our weary hearts with the strength we need for the Christian life.

When we speak of Jesus nourishing us at the Lord's Supper, we need to be clear about what that *doesn't* mean. Some Christian traditions teach that the Lord's Supper miraculously heals believers from physical ailments. Others teach that something magical happens simply by eating the bread and drinking the cup. Such superstitious views of the Supper are wrong. Scripture clearly teaches that the bread and wine are *symbols* that point to a greater reality; they're not magical items in themselves. Nor does the Bible promise physical healing through the Supper. Instead, we encounter Jesus spiritually and our faith is strengthened as we trust in his covenant promises.

How should this affect how you view the Lord's Supper? Here are a few thoughts:

- Ask Jesus to remind you of his sacrifice on your behalf.
- Believe that Jesus will supply you with the grace that you need to grow in trusting him and obeying his commands.
- Come to the Lord's Supper expectantly: together with your church family, you are coming to a meal like no other, *a meal with Jesus himself.*

A Meal for Reflection

A few years ago, I, along with other religious leaders in my country, was invited to an important event—a meal at the palace of a Sheikh. This extra-special event required IDs and passports submitted ahead of time. We submitted to security checks and a very particular decorum. Nobody could just waltz into this meal!

Who's the Lord's Supper for? And what are the requirements to participate? So far, we've seen that the Lord's Supper is a meal for Jesus's family in which we remember our Savior's death as we commune with both Jesus and one another.

But when we take the Lord's Supper, we need to recognize that we're dining with *royalty*; we need to remember we're seated at the table of King Jesus himself! Like any meal with royalty, there are requirements and restrictions.

Once again, let's go back to Corinth, where Paul instructed the church on how they ought to celebrate the Lord's Supper. If you remember the context, the Corinthian Christians were treating each other poorly by coming to the Lord's Supper in sinful gluttony. Paul exhorted them to examine themselves beforehand:

> Whoever, therefore, eats the bread or drinks the cup of the Lord in an unworthy manner will be guilty concerning the body and blood of the Lord. Let a person examine himself, then, and so eat of the bread and drink of the cup. For anyone who eats and drinks without discerning the body eats and drinks judgment on himself. That is why many of you are weak and ill, and some have died. But if we judged ourselves truly, we would not be judged. But when we are judged by the Lord, we are disciplined so that we may not be condemned along with the world.
>
> So then, my brothers, when you come together to eat, wait for one another—if anyone is hungry, let him eat at home—so that when you come together it will not be for judgment. (1 Cor. 11:27–34)

Those are serious words! This isn't any ordinary meal. This is a meal with royalty; it's the family table of Jesus our King. When the Corinthians disregarded one another at the Lord's Supper, God judged and disciplined them with sickness and even death. That's how seriously Jesus takes this meal.

We ought to take it seriously as well. How do we do that? First, we need to recognize the restrictions on who can and cannot participate. Second, we need to consider what's required for those who do participate.

1) Restrictions

Since the Lord's Supper is Jesus's family meal, those who participate in it must be part of Jesus's family. This means that there are three restrictions around who can come to the table: belief, baptism, and belonging. Let's look at each.

Belief

The Lord's Supper is for *believers* in Jesus: those who have repented of their sins and trusted in

Jesus for eternal life. Non-Christians cannot participate in this meal because they haven't trusted in Jesus's death for their forgiveness—they're not a part of his family. They can't *remember* Jesus's death because they haven't trusted its significance for their lives.

Baptism

The Lord's Supper is for those who have been baptized. Not only should someone have trusted in Christ, they should have publicly identified with him and his family through baptism. As already noted, baptism and the Lord's Supper are both signs of the new covenant: baptism is the *initial* sign of the covenant, and the Lord's Supper is the *ongoing* sign. Baptism is how you enter the King's palace, which is necessary *before* you sit down at the King's table.

Belonging

The Lord's Supper is for members in "good standing" of a local church. Why this restriction? Recall what we discussed previously:

membership in a local church isn't optional for the Christian life; it's the context in which we live out our commitment to Jesus and his people. So before you sit at the family dinner table, you should make sure you've committed yourself to be a part of the family—a commitment that's made through membership.

We've also seen that the Lord's Supper is how local churches identify who belongs to Jesus's family and who doesn't. How? Well, Jesus commands churches to ensure that nobody merely gives him lip service by claiming to follow him while disobeying his commands. Jesus instructs churches to guard their holiness and witness. They do this by practicing church discipline.

Church discipline is how a church corrects and confronts sin in its midst (see Matt. 18:15–20 and 1 Cor. 5:1–13).[4] If someone claims to follow Jesus but continues living in unrepentant sin, God commands his people to remove that person from membership and exclude them from the Lord's Supper. This act is called *excommunication* because it means being put out of communion. The goal of this difficult act is to awaken the person to the seriousness of the sin so that he or she would turn from it. Nevertheless, the implication for the Lord's Supper is clear: only members in good standing (i.e., not under church discipline) may participate.

Typically, when a church celebrates the Lord's Supper, the pastor or person leading the service will explain these restrictions so that non-Christian visitors or others who do not qualify will not participate.

So should you participate in the Lord's Supper? Ask yourself these four questions, and if the answer to all four of them is yes, then you're good to go!

- Have I *turned from my sin* and *trusted* in Jesus and his sacrificial death for me?
- Have I *identified* with Jesus and his people through baptism?
- Have I *committed* myself to Jesus and his people through membership in a local church?
- Am I currently *walking in fellowship* with Jesus's family in the local church?

2) Requirements

God's word restricts who can and can't participate in the Lord's Supper. But it doesn't stop there. It also places certain requirements on those who do participate. To understand these requirements, we need to consider what Paul says in 1 Corinthians 11:27–34, particularly what he means when he says that a person must "examine himself," that we must "judge ourselves truly," and that we must "discern the body."

Once again, let's remember the context. In Corinth, people were disregarding their fellow church members by gorging on food and getting drunk on wine so that nothing was left when the poorer church members showed up. These rich gluttons were dishonoring their fellow church members. Instead of being a time to celebrate family bonds in Christ, the Corinthian Lord's Supper became a time of division in the body of Christ.

So, first and foremost, Paul's instructions pertain to our concern for fellow church members. When we come to the Lord's Supper, we come in unity with our brothers and sisters in Christ. We're members of the same body, and Jesus has made us so through his body and blood. We cannot claim to be *remembering* Christ's sacrifice at the Lord's Supper without *recognizing* how that sacrifice unites us to one another. In fact, to despise fellow church members at the Lord's Supper is to despise the Lord's death and even to despise the Lord himself. That's what it means to eat and drink "without discerning the body" (1 Cor. 11:29). So the primary requirement when we come to the Lord's Supper is to ensure that we are doing so with due regard and love for our brothers and sisters in Christ.

The Lord's Supper also requires us to examine ourselves. Some Christians have misunderstood Paul's command not to participate in an "unworthy manner." They take this self-examination a bit too far and get worried they've unknowingly committed some sin that's made them unworthy. But sin is a reality in all of our lives; none of us can claim "worthiness" on the basis of what we've done or haven't done. Brothers and sisters, don't fall into paralysis by self-analysis.

On the other hand, self-examination is healthy and helpful if done in light of the gospel. Our lives are often busy and noisy; the Lord's Supper gives us the opportunity to slow down, reflect, and consider our hearts. Each time we come to the table, we're given the opportunity to revive our faith in Jesus, and to strengthen our resolve to walk in repentance, holiness, and love.

Now that we've looked at those requirements for participation in the Lord's Supper, you're ready to think about how you can best prepare for the meal. Here are a few questions to ask:

- Am I trusting in anything other than Jesus and his death to save me from sin? If the answer is yes, now's a good time to renew your faith in Jesus as your only hope in life and death.
- Are there sins I need to confess and repent of before the Lord? If the answer is yes, now's a good time to confess your sins to God, receive his forgiveness, and resolve to walk in repentance.

- Am I living in peace and unity with my brothers and sisters in Christ? If the answer is no, then be sure to pursue peace and reconciliation in any broken relationships *before* you participate in the Lord's Supper (read Matt. 5:21–24).

Several years ago, two women in our church had gotten into a dispute. Before the Lord's Supper, the pastor encouraged us to examine ourselves and participate in a worthy manner. I distinctly remember how one of these women walked to the other end of the hall to the woman she had offended. They shared a long hug with tears streaming down their faces. They reconciled with one another and took the Lord's Supper as sisters in Christ, recognizing that they could forgive one another because of what this meal represented—that the Lord Jesus, through his death, had forgiven them.

A Meal of Anticipation

I love cooking, especially big, hearty Indian meals, and inviting people over to share dinner with my family. Cooking a big Indian meal is an "event," something that involves several hours of careful labor. As I cook, the anticipation and excitement in my home increases as my family members get little previews of what's to come. A spoonful of curry here, a little piece of meat there, the aromas wafting through the air—all of it increases the *oohs!* and the *aahs!* as everyone waits to finally be seated at the table where they can dig in.

As Jesus ate his final Passover meal with his disciples, he told them about another meal he was eagerly awaiting:

> I tell you I will not drink again of this fruit of the vine until that day when I drink it new with you in my Father's kingdom. (Matt. 26:29)

Even as Jesus instituted the Lord's Supper, he wanted his disciples to know that this meal was only a preview, a foretaste, of a greater meal to come.

The goal of the Christian life is ultimately fellowship—*communion*—with God. Our lives right now should be filled with anticipation, hope, and longing as we await the glories of God's new creation. The Bible tells us that there is coming a day when God will make all things new, a time when all our sorrows and trials will end, and we will enjoy fellowship with God forever (Rev. 21:3–4). On that day, Jesus, the bridegroom, will be finally and forever united to his blood-bought bride, the church (Rev. 21:2, 9). The Savior will be forever united to the people he shed his blood to save.

Scripture repeatedly reminds us that this glorious day will be celebrated with a wedding feast in honor of the Lamb and his Bride:

> Then I heard what seemed to be the voice of a great multitude, like the roar of many waters and like the sound of mighty peals of thunder, crying out,
>
> > "Hallelujah!
> > For the Lord our God
> >   the Almighty reigns.
> > Let us rejoice and exult

and give him the glory,
for the marriage of the Lamb has
    come,
    and his Bride has made herself
    ready;
it was granted her to clothe herself
    with fine linen, bright and
    pure"—
for the fine linen is the righteous
    deeds of the saints.

And the angel said to me, "Write this:
Blessed are those who are invited to the
marriage supper of the Lamb." And he said
to me, "These are the true words of God."
(Rev. 19:6–9; see also Isa. 25:6–9)

The Lord's Supper is a foretaste of this moment, a lick of the spoon. It's meant to whet our appetites for the feast that represents the final fulfillment of all God's saving promises. That's why the apostle Paul says, "For as often as you eat this bread and drink the cup, you proclaim the Lord's death *until he comes*" (1 Cor. 11:26). When we eat and drink at the Lord's Supper, we're not just anticipating, we're also proclaiming Jesus's coming kingdom. We're not just proclaiming that Jesus died, but also that he's risen and coming again. We're proclaiming in the present not merely what Jesus has done in the past, but also what he will do in the future. We eat and drink as we anticipate the glorious day when we will eat with him in his heavenly kingdom.

And guess what? Jesus is eagerly looking forward to that meal just as much as we do. The joyful bridegroom is longing to be united with his bride.

A Quick Review

We've covered quite a bit of ground in this little booklet. Here's a quick, five-point summary of what we're doing at the Lord's Supper[5]:

1) We look *backward*: we remember Christ's body and blood given for us at the cross; we remember that his death has brought us forgiveness and eternal life.
2) We look *outward*: we celebrate the family bond we share with brothers and sisters in Christ in the local church.

3) We look *upward*: we realize that we're lifted up to be seated with Jesus our heavenly host, the one to whom we bring our hungry hearts for nourishment with the grace of the new covenant.

4) We look *inward*: we examine our hearts to ensure that we're walking in faith and repentance, and living with love for our brothers and sisters in Christ.

5) We look *forward*: we wait in hope for the glorious day when we will celebrate the fulfillment of all God's promises at his heavenly banquet.

Recommended Resources

My thoughts in this book were shaped by a number of very helpful works on the Lord's Supper, which I commend to you for further study.

Beginner

Bobby Jamieson. *Understanding the Lord's Supper*. Nashville: B&H Publishing, 2016.

R. C. Sproul. *What Is the Lord's Supper?* Sanford, FL: Reformation Trust, 2013.

Intermediate

John S. Hammett. *40 Questions about Baptism and the Lord's Supper*. Grand Rapids, MI: Kregel, 2015.

Robert Letham. *The Lord's Supper: Eternal Word in Broken Bread*. Phillipsburg, NJ: P&R, 2001.

Keith A. Mathison. *The Lord's Supper: Answers to Common Questions*. Sanford, FL: Reformation Trust, 2019.

Guy P. Waters. *The Lord's Supper as the Sign and the Meal of the New Covenant*. Wheaton, IL: Crossway, 2019.

Advanced

Thomas R. Schreiner and Matthew R. Crawford, eds. *The Lord's Supper: Remembering and Proclaiming Christ until He Comes*. Nashville: B&H Academic, 2010.

Thomas Watson. *The Mystery of the Lord's Supper*. Louisville, KY: GLH Publishing, 2014.

Notes

1. This idea that the Lord's Supper is a meal of *remem-brance* is quite different from what some church tra-ditions teach. Roman Catholics teach that the bread and wine mysteriously transform into Christ's actual body and blood. They believe that Christ's sacrifice must be literally "re-presented" on the altar. But this is incorrect, because the Bible teaches that Jesus's death on the cross was a once-for-all offering to cleanse us from sin: "we have been sanctified through the offering of the body of Jesus Christ once for all" (Heb. 10:10). There's no biblical basis to think that Jesus wanted his disciples to eat his literal body and blood.

   If you're a gospel-believing Christian wondering if it's okay for you to participate in the Lord's Supper at Roman Catholic Mass, let me offer some advice: don't. The Roman Catholic teaching on the Lord's Supper denies that Jesus's one-time sacrificial offering on the cross was sufficient to take away our sins. Instead, they believe he must be offered again and again in the Lord's

Supper. This teaching denies the heart of the gospel. By participating in the bread and wine at Catholic Mass, we give our approval to a false understanding of the gospel. This is why many Protestant Reformers were willing to be martyred rather than take the mass and affirm the Roman Catholic teaching on the Lord's Supper.

2. For more information, see Mark Dever, *Why Should I Join a Church?* (Wheaton, IL: Crossway, 2020).

3. Churches who affirm this principle differ on whether to make an exception for those who are physically unable to attend church due to disability or age (e.g., those who are homebound or in a nursing home). Those who would disallow such a practice believe that one's physical inability to participate in the Supper excuses them from the command. Those who permit this would say that it is allowable if administered by representatives from the church as a special exception that is not normative or ordinary.

4. For more information on church discipline, see Jonathan Leeman, *Is It Loving to Practice Church Discipline?* (Wheaton, IL: Crossway, 2020).

5. After developing this five-point summary myself, I saw that two other writers had also used similar summaries to describe the Lord's Supper: Erik Raymond, "What Should I Think about During the Lord's Supper?" The Gospel Coalition (blog), April 16, 2019, https://www.the gospelcoalition.org/blogs/erik-raymond/think-lords -supper/ and Bobby Jamieson, *Understanding the Lord's Supper* (Nashville: B&H Publishing, 2016), 63–66.

Scripture Index

IX 9Marks

Building Healthy Churches

9Marks exists to equip church leaders with a biblical vision and practical resources for displaying God's glory to the nations through healthy churches.

To that end, we want to see churches characterized by these nine marks of health:

1. Expositional Preaching
2. Gospel Doctrine
3. A Biblical Understanding of Conversion and Evangelism
4. Biblical Church Membership
5. Biblical Church Discipline
6. A Biblical Concern for Discipleship and Growth
7. Biblical Church Leadership
8. A Biblical Understanding of the Practice of Prayer
9. A Biblical Understanding and Practice of Missions

Find all our Crossway titles and other resources at 9Marks.org.

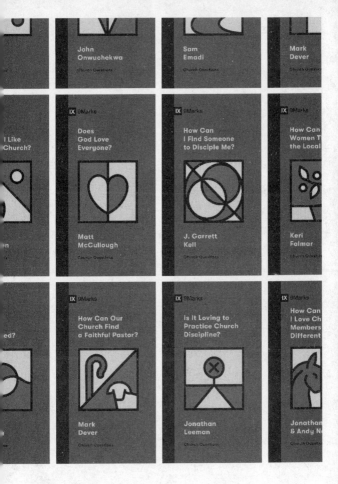

John Onwuchekwa

Sam Emadi

Mark Dever

I Like Church?

Does God Love Everyone?
Matt McCullough

How Can I Find Someone to Disciple Me?
J. Garrett Kell

How Can Women T the Local
Keri Folmar

How Can Our Church Find a Faithful Pastor?
Mark Dever

Is It Loving to Practice Church Discipline?
Jonathan Leeman

How Can I Love Ch Members Different
Jonathan & Andy N

IX 9Marks Church Questions

Providing ordinary Christians with sound and accessible biblical teaching by answering common questions about church life.

For more information, visit crossway.org.